How Does Weather Happen?

How Come It's Raining?

Judith Williams

Enslow Elementary
an imprint of
Enslow Publishers, Inc.

40 Industrial Road
Box 398
Berkeley Heights, NJ 07922
USA

http://www.enslow.com

Words to Know

cycle (SY cuhl)—A group of things that happen over and over in the same order.

droplet—A tiny drop of liquid. Droplets are much smaller than raindrops.

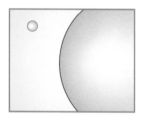

liquid (LIH kwid)—Something wet that can flow, such as water.

rain gauge (RAYN GAYJ)—A container that has a ruler to measure rain.

water vapor (WAH tur VAY pur)—Water that has turned into a gas, such as fog.

Contents

What do raindrops look like?

Do they look like teardrops? No!

Raindrops can be two shapes.

Small drops are round. Large drops start out round, but flatten as they fall. They are shaped like hamburgers!

Where do raindrops come from?

Raindrops are part of Earth's water cycle. The water cycle starts with the sun.

The sun heats Earth's air, land, and water. Water is in soil, plants, rivers, and oceans.

Some of the water changes into a gas called water vapor. It rises into the sky. You cannot see water vapor.

When water vapor cools,
you can see it. Fog is
water vapor that cooled
close to the ground.

What happens to the water vapor?

Water vapor rises into the sky. The higher it goes, the cooler it gets.

When the water vapor cools, some of it changes into a liquid again. You see this liquid water in the sky as clouds.

Are clouds made of water?

Yes, but clouds are not like big puddles in the sky.

Clouds are really made of many, many small water **droplets**.

The droplets form around very tiny things that float in the air. They form around small bits of salt, dust, and soil that are blowing around.

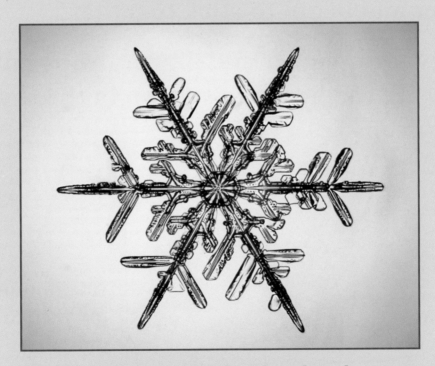

If it is cold enough, the droplets become tiny pieces of ice instead.

How do droplets become raindrops?

Inside clouds, the air and droplets move around. The droplets bang into each other and begin to stick together.

They form bigger and bigger drops until they are too heavy to stay up in the sky. The drops fall as rain.

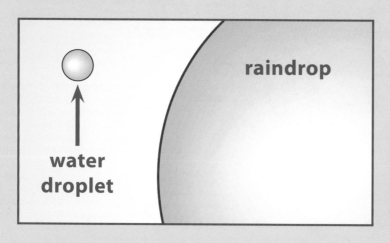

water droplet

raindrop

One raindrop is made up of millions of water droplets.

Does every cloud bring rain?

No. Most clouds go up and down, up and down for days—without ever raining on anyone!

Dark clouds that are low in the sky hold the most water. They are the ones that often rain on us.

Once it starts to rain, we can measure how much rain is falling.

How is rain measured?

Rain is measured using a **rain gauge**. Rain falls into the open top of the gauge.

There is a tool inside the rain gauge. It measures how much rain fell.

rain gauge

People keep records of how much rain falls every day, week, and year in places all over the world.

Places with the most rainfall in the world are Hawaii, Colombia, and India.

What happens to the rain after it falls?

Rain fills rivers, lakes, and oceans. It sinks into the ground, too. Some underground water flows back into the oceans.

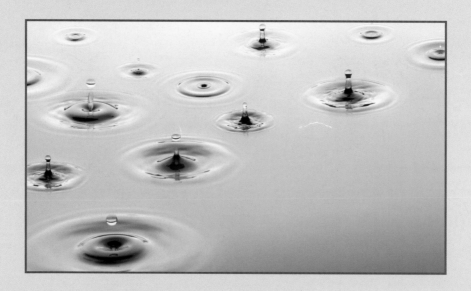

Clouds

Rain

Water vapor rises.

Ocean

When the sun shines again, more water turns to water vapor. Then the water cycle begins all over again. Even on sunny days, raindrops are getting ready to fall!

How much rain has fallen?

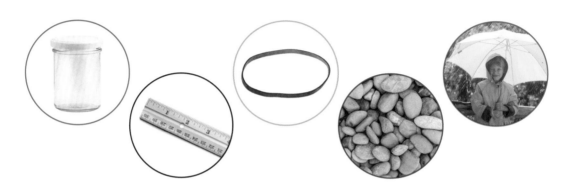

You will need:

- ☑ **a glass jar with a wide mouth (The sides of the jar should be straight up and down.)**
- ☑ **a 12-inch ruler**
- ☑ **a rubber band**
- ☑ **rocks**
- ☑ **a rainy day**

1. Carefully put the rubber band around the jar.

2. Slide the ruler between the rubber band and the jar so that the numbers face out.

3. Put the jar outside in the rain. Push some rocks against the jar so that it will not fall over if the wind blows.

4. When it stops raining, look at the jar. How much rain has fallen? Use the ruler to measure the amount.

Learn More

Bauer, Marion Dane. *Rain.* New York: Aladdin, 2003.

Branley, Franklyn. *Down Comes the Rain.* New York: HarperCollins Publishers, 1997.

Sherman, Josepha. *Splish! Splash! A Book About Rain.* Minneapolis, Minn.: Picture Window Books, 2003.

Waldman, Meil. *The Snowflake: A Water Cycle Story.* Brookfield, Conn.: Millbrook Press, 2003.

Williams, Judith. *Searching for Stormy Weather With a Scientist.* Berkeley Heights, N.J.: Enslow Publishers, Inc., 2004.

Index

Enslow Elementary, an imprint of Enslow Publishers, Inc.
Enslow Elementary® is a registered trademark of Enslow Publishers, Inc.

Copyright © 2015 by Enslow Publishers, Inc.

Originally published as *Why Is It Raining?* in 2005.

All rights reserved.

No part of this book may be reproduced by any means without the written permission of the publisher.

Library of Congress Cataloging-in-Publication Data

Williams, Judith.
  How come it's raining? / Judith Williams.
    p. cm. — (How does weather happen?)
  Includes bibliographical reference and index.
  Summary: "Explains in simple terms the science behind rain and includes a glossary and the water cycle" —Provided by publisher.
  ISBN 978-0-7660-6380-8
  1. Rain and rainfall—Juvenile literature. I. Title.
  QC924.7 W55 2015
  551.57'7—dc23

              2004016789

Future Editions:
Paperback ISBN: 978-0-7660-6381-5
Single-User PDF ISBN: 978-0-7660-6383-9
EPUB ISBN: 978-0-7660-6382-2
Multi-User PDF ISBN: 978-0-7660-6384-6

Printed in the United States of America

102014 Bang Printing, Brainerd, Minn.

10 9 8 7 6 5 4 3 2 1

To Our Readers: We have done our best to make sure all Internet addresses in this book were active and appropriate when we went to press. However, the author and the publisher have no control over and assume no liability for the material available on those Internet sites or on other Web sites they may link to. Any comments or suggestions can be sent by e-mail to comments@enslow.com or to the address on the back cover.

♻ Enslow Publishers, Inc., is committed to printing our books on recycled paper. The paper in every book contains 10% to 30% post-consumer waste (PCW). The cover board on the outside of each book contains 100% PCW. Our goal is to do our part to help young people and the environment, too!

Every effort has been made to locate all copyright holders of material used in this book. If any errors or omissions have occurred, corrections will be made in future editions of this book.

Interior Photo Credits: © 1996–2004 Jupiterimages, p. 20 (last); © 2004 Jupiterimages, p. 15; Artville LLC, p. 17; Enslow Publishers, Inc., pp. 2 (second), 12. Shutterstock.com: Antonov Roman, p. 18; BigBigbb1, p. 20 (fourth); bikeriderlondon, p. 13; Eldad Carin, p. 20 (third); Fztommy, p. 7; ievgen sosnytskyi, p. 9; Jaroslav Bartoš, p. 23; Kichigin, p. 11; Mega Pixel, p. 20 (second); Ovocheva, p. 1 (weather icons); Patrick Foto, p. 5; Pizla09, pp. 2 (third), 4; Steve Heap, pp. 2 (fourth), 16; Sundraw Photography, p. 1 (flowers); unclenikola, p. 20 (first); Vibrant Image Studio, p. 10. Tom LaBaff, pp. 2 (first and last), 19.

Cover Credit: Shutterstock.com: Ovocheva (weather icons); Patrick Foto (girl with umbrella).

Series Literacy Consultant

Allan A. De Fina, Ph.D.
Past President of the
New Jersey Reading Association
Professor, Department of
Literacy Education
New Jersey City University

Science Consultant

Harold Brooks, Ph.D.
NOAA/National Severe
Storms Laboratory
Norman, Oklahoma

Note to Parents and Teachers: The **How Does Weather Happen?** series supports the National Science Education Standards for K–4 science. The "Words to Know" section introduces subject-specific vocabulary words, including pronunciation and definitions. Early readers may need help with these new words.